Multiple Mini Interview for Medical School:
Practice Interview Series
Exam 1

Multiple Mini Interview for Medical School: Practice Interview Series Exam 1

Jordan Westley

Copyright © 2020 by Jordan Westley

All rights reserved.

No part of this book may be reproduced in any form or by any electronic or mechanical means including information storage and retrieval systems, without permission in writing from the author. The only exception is by a reviewer, who may quote short excerpts in a review.

Printed in Canada

Table of Contents

Instructions for Interviewer 7

Instructions for Timer 7

   Timing Schedule in Brief 7

Equipment 8

Full Length MMI Practice Exam 1 11

Comments for MMI Questions 45

Interviewer Scoring Sheets 53

More Resources 57

   Multiple Mini Interview for Medical School: Practice Interview Series 57

   Medical School Multiple Mini Interview: The Essentials 59

Instructions for Interviewer

The practice interview should be done in a quiet room. Remove the interviewer scoring sheets at the end of the book. The role of timer may be performed by the interviewer or assistant. Instructions for the timer are below. The applicant should be outside the room and has 2 minutes to read the question. The applicant enters the room when a buzzer signaling the end of the 2 minutes. The 2-minute signal is performed by the timer or interviewer. When the applicant enters the room, greet the applicant. Make sure the applicant has read the question and invite the applicant to answer the question. When the applicant finishes answering the question or at the request of the applicant, you may ask the prompting questions written on the page after the interview question. If there is still time, invite the applicant to add more information, otherwise you are not allowed to engage in small talk with the applicant. You may need to remain silent or remind the applicant that you are not allowed to talk outside of the question or offer more information on the question. You can let the applicant read the question again and invite them to provide more information. A one-minute warning buzzer is sounded by the timer a minute before the end of the 8 minutes allotted for the question. Then at 8 minutes, a buzzer is sounded by the timer to signal the end of the question. At the end of the question, the applicant leaves the room and the interviewer will provide the gradings and comments on the interviewer scoring sheet provided. While the interviewer is filling out the interviewer score sheet, the applicant leaves the room to read the next question outside the room. Repeat for each question until all the questions have been answered.

Instructions for Timer

1. Press the buzzer to start the interview.
2. Wait for 2 minutes and press the buzzer. Wait for 7 minutes and press the buzzer. Wait for 1 minute and press the buzzer. Repeat step 2 until all the questions have been answered.

Timing Schedule in Brief

- 2 minutes to read the question

- 8 minutes to answer the question. There is a warning buzzer a minute before the end of the 8 minutes allotted to answer the question.

Equipment
- MMI Questions found in this book
- MMI Interviewer Scoring Sheets found at the end of this book
- Pencil
- Timer

FULL LENGTH MMI PRACTICE EXAM

Full Length MMI Practice Exam 1

Below is a practice multiple mini interview that mimics the type of questions, duration and number of questions you would expect in an MMI.

Instructions:

There are eight questions. You have two minutes to read and think about the question and eight minutes to answer the question. Flip to the next page to view the prompting questions. Prompting questions are available on the next page and should be consulted when necessary. In the actual exam, the interviewer will read the prompting questions when you've finished answering before the time limit or if you request for the prompting questions.

Flip the page to begin.

Q1.
You are a security guard at a golf tournament that is raising money for cystic fibrosis. The tournament is being sponsored by a large company. On your shift a noisy person and his friends walk around drunk, loud and is disrupting other players. That person is the son of the major sponsoring company's owner for the golf tournament.

What would you do in this situation?

Q1. Prompting Questions

   A. The sponsor's son tells you to mind your own business or he'll tell his dad to fire you. What would you do?

   B. He reminds you that his father is sponsoring the event and that if he isn't happy his father can withdraw his support and this event may not occur in the future. How do you respond?

   C. What factors do you need to consider in making your decision for action?

Q2.
The Heart and Stroke Foundation asserts that cardiovascular diseases are the number one killer in North America. A think tank is considering implementing a cardiovascular health tax on food that increases risk of cardiovascular diseases. The money collected from this new health tax will be placed into cardiovascular health research and hospitals to improve treatment and health of North Americans. Do you think this new health tax should be implemented?

Q2. Prompting Questions

A. What are the benefits of this health tax?

B. What are considerations in implementing such a tax?

C. What are the drawbacks of implementing such a tax?

D. What are the consequences of implementing this tax?

Q3.

You are visiting your grandfather and you tell him that you've been volunteering at a hospital and you're considering being a doctor. He's proud of you for wanting to work in a caring profession. He remembers when he was in a hospital 40 years ago and says that it must be very different nowadays. What changes have been made in today's hospital as oppose to 40 years ago?

Q3. Prompting Questions

A. Describe the current hospital settings.

B. What would be different in hospitals 40 years ago?

C. What do you think hospitals will be like in the future?

Q4.
You are conducting medical research at the university. The laboratory focuses on researching medication that will prolong lifespan. You discovered in your project a drug candidate that may double a person's life span. The drug has only been shown in rats and the results are clear and there are no visible side effects. You are curious if the effect will translate into humans. Would you try the drug yourself?

Q4. Prompting Questions

A. What would you gain for taking the drug?

B. What are some possible consequences of taking the drug?

C. If the drug does prolong human life spans, what would happen to society?

Q5.

Most of the clinical trials are performed in countries outside of North America. But most of the medications are prescribed in North America. Do you think this is approach to clinical trials should be modified?

Q5. Prompting Questions

A. What are the benefits of conducting clinical trials abroad?

B. What are some problems of testing drugs abroad?

Q6.
You are a family physician in a rural town. You have a patient who needs surgery at a major hospital. The closest town is 700 km away. How would you transport the patient?

Q6. Prompting Questions

A. What are the factors you need to consider?

B. How can you transport the patient to the nearest major hospital?

C. What would you do if there was a snow storm and there is no way you can take the patient to the nearest hospital?

Q7.
You are living with an exchange student from Japan and he is having trouble understanding the difference between "cool" as a temperature and as a description of a person that doesn't mean getting hypothermia. They also don't understand how a drink can be "hot" and a person can be "hot" but not have a fever. How can you help them understand many of these common colloquiums in English?

Q7. Prompting Questions

A. How does the Japanese exchange student feel in not understanding common colloquiums in English?

B. What are some factors you need to consider in helping him?

C. How can you help him?

Q8.
You have an appointment with a group of friends. You're just on your way to meet up with your friends when your younger brother needs help for his physics homework. He has an exam coming up. What would you do in this situation?

Q8. Prompting Questions

A. How does your brother feel?

B. How will your friends feel?

C. What can you do to help your brother study for physics?

Comments for MMI Questions

Each MMI question is made to be open ended and can encompass a wide range of answers that are unique to each person. There are a few areas to note in providing your answers that will lead you to fulfill the points that the interviewer is expecting and evaluating. Comments are provided for each of the questions in the practice interviews.

Exam 1

Q1.
   Question:

   You are a security guard at a golf tournament that is raising money for cystic fibrosis. The tournament is being sponsored by a large company. On your shift a noisy person and his friends walk around drunk, loud and is disrupting other players. That person is the son of the major sponsoring company's owner for the golf tournament.

   What would you do in this situation?

Comments:

This question tests the integrity and ability of the applicant to respond and maintain priorities in a stressful scenario. Tact is needed to take into consideration disruption to the event and maintaining congenial relations with the sponsor.

Q2.
Question:
The Heart and Stroke Foundation asserts that cardiovascular diseases are the number one killer in North America. A think tank is considering implementing a cardiovascular health tax on food that increases risk of cardiovascular diseases. The money collected from this new health tax will be placed into cardiovascular health research and hospitals to improve treatment and health of North Americans. Do you think this new health tax should be implemented?

Comments:
Implementing a tax on food that increases the risk of cardiovascular diseases would set a precedent for implementing taxes on other diseases. Deciding on where to draw the line would be difficult because this could lead to a slippery slope. Discerning which foods increase cardiovascular disease risk would be difficult. There may not be unanimous agreement on certain foods. Assigning a risk level on food items would require a criteria and ranking system that may not be linear and will be difficult. A consideration is the extent of government's ability to control or interfere with lifestyle choices and infringing on individual rights. There is incomplete information on cardiovascular disease risks and implementing a national program prematurely may have harmful and unexpected consequences. For example, alcohol was known to be harmful to

health and increases the risk for cardiovascular disease. But later an ingredient in red wine was discovered to improve cardiovascular health and even extends life span.

Q3.

Question:
You are visiting your grandfather and you tell him that you've been volunteering at a hospital and you're considering being a doctor. He's proud of you for wanting to work in a caring profession. He remembers when he was in a hospital 40 years ago and says that it must be very different nowadays. What changes have been made in today's hospital as oppose to 40 years ago?

Comments:
Hospitals are designed to be more logistically efficient by placing sections of the hospital that interact frequently together. Hospitals are also being designed to increase the sense of wellbeing and ease of navigation by making the hospital feel less like a hospital. For example, there are hospitals that are designed to reflect a shopping mall because the layout is familiar to most people, comfortable and easy to navigate. Hospitals in the past were much smaller than hospitals of the present. You can see some hospitals that have wings added to the original hospitals. These additions more than double the size of the original hospital. The architecture of old hospitals is mainly brick and mortar. New hospitals are designed with glass and metal to increase natural sunlight while providing a more modern design. The use of computers to record patient information did not exist four decades ago. Computers will continue to play a greater role in medicine. We're creating electronic health records and is a major innovation in the health care system. Some doctors will

communicate with their patients through e-mail and this was unheard of in the past. In the future, it is likely that doctors will be communicating more with their patients electronically.

Q4.

Question:
You are conducting medical research at the university. The laboratory focuses on researching medication that will prolong lifespan. You discovered in your project a drug candidate that may double a person's life span. The drug has only been shown in rats and the results are clear and there are no visible side effects. You are curious if the effect will translate into humans. Would you try the drug yourself?

Comments:
Many drug discoveries were performed by the researcher testing the drug on themselves including LSD. If the drug had no significant side effects, you'll be the first person to try the drug, provide valuable information on the drug and may even fast track the drug to market. However, the effects on humans are unknown and the side effects are unknown. If the drug is successful, humans may live twice as long, each person's productive years will double. Some consequences would be increases in health care costs as people live longer and need more health care services. The talent pool of skilled labor will increase as more people are able to work longer, practice longer and gain more experience. Retirement age will be changed to an older age and pension packages will be modified.

Q5.

Question:
Most of the clinical trials are performed in countries outside of North America. But most of the medications are prescribed in

North America. Do you think this is approach to clinical trials should be modified?

Comments:
Clinical trials conducted abroad reduce the cost for drug companies. People in some countries are more willing to sign up for clinical trials which results in quicker recruitment. The benefits are lower costs for clinical trials. Lower costs provide more capital to investigate other drug candidates. Lower costs allow more drugs to be investigated which increases potential drug discoveries to treat patients. Clinical trials require many years and recruiting subjects can sometimes be difficult. So quicker recruitment will quicken clinical trials and result in drugs reaching the market faster. Some problems with testing drugs abroad is data collected from these clinical trials will be tested on people of a different race from most North Americans. The effects of the drug may be different due to subtle genetic differences which may cause side effects, decreased efficacy or even possibilities of decrease metabolism that can lead to drug overdose. There are also problems of providing compensation to subjects abroad that are a fraction of a North American subject which would be unfair. In addition, it would be unfair for people in other countries to carry more of the risks associated with clinical trials. Clinical trials currently meet the FDA regulations but amendments to improve fairness and better North American representation in clinical trial data would improve safety for patients and quality of clinical trials.

Q6.
Question:
You are a family physician in a rural town. You have a patient who needs surgery at a major hospital. The closest town is 700 km away. How would you transport the patient?

Comments:
The first thing would be to contact the nearest hospital and arrange for the patient to be transferred to the nearest hospital. You can brainstorm ways to transport the patient and can include ambulance, car, helicopter, plane, bus, train, and etc. If there is no way the patient can be taken out of the town, you would need to ensure the safety of the patient. Contact the surgeon in the major hospital to take steps to prepare the patient for surgery. Monitor and maintain the health of the patient. Make arrangements to transport the patient to a major hospital once the snow storm clears.

Q7.

Question:
You are living with an exchange student from Japan and he is having trouble understanding the difference between "cool" as a temperature and as a description of a person that doesn't mean getting hypothermia. They also don't understand how a drink can be "hot" and a person can be "hot" but not have a fever. How can you help them understand many of these common colloquiums in English?

Comments:
He may feel frustrated that he can't understand something. He may be embarrassed for not knowing something that is common in English and not wanting to bother someone to repeatedly explain the same thing. He could be disappointed in himself for not getting it. There may be some cultural factors such as feelings of shame, dishonor or possibility of losing face that might be taken into account. You can help him by making him feel comfortable. Provide a supportive environment for him to learn. Learning a foreign language can be a scary experience. He

can feel safe in exposing areas of weakness or uncertainty. He should feel comfortable being vulnerable to allow himself to learn from native speakers. You can help him by providing further examples of colloquiums, write down examples, and point out examples during your daily conversations. You can provide resources such as books, DVD's, CD's, websites, software programs, movies, and TV shows.

Q8.

Question:
You have an appointment with a group of friends. You're just on your way to meet up with your friends when your younger brother needs help for his physics homework. He has an exam coming up. What would you do in this situation?

Comments:
Your brother probably feels desperate because his exam is coming up and he is still struggling with his homework. Also, he probably feels stressed that the exam is looming over him. Your friends will probably feel impatient if you're late and angry if you did not let them know. But will feel respected and content if you notify them that you'll be late or unable to come because you need to help your brother study. You can help him by explaining physics concepts, guide him through homework problems, give him pointers on writing exams, provide extra practice problems to solidify concepts and difficult topics. Answer questions carefully and patiently, offer encouragement to boost his self confidence.

Interviewer Scoring Sheets

Instructions:

Cut out the interviewer score sheets. The interviewer uses the score sheets to evaluate and grade the applicant's performance. The interviewer will provide a grade from a scale of 1 to 10 ranging from poor to excellent for each category and an overall score. Space is provided under each category to note areas of strength, challenges, and improvements.

Exam 1

Date: _____

Communication skills:

Question #:	1	2	3	4	5	6	7	8
Score (__/10)								

Strength of Arguments:

Question #:	1	2	3	4	5	6	7	8
Score (__/10)								

Suitability for Health Sciences:

Question #:	1	2	3	4	5	6	7	8
Score (__/10)								

Overall:

Question #:	1	2	3	4	5	6	7	8
Score (__/10)								

More Resources

Multiple Mini Interview for Medical School: Practice Interview Series
By Jordan Westley

More Medical School MMI Practice Interview Exams

Practicing the multiple mini interview is essential to the success of the applicant. A full-length practice interview simulates the experience of the multiple mini interview. It prepares the applicant for the types of questions, stamina, and experience of the multiple medical interview. Review the marking sheets and discussions to gain insight from the interviewer's perspective. Practicing the interview experience helps prepare you to be confident and comfortable with the multiple mini interview.

Multiple Mini Interview for Medical School: Practice Interview Series Exam 1 by Jordan Westley

Multiple Mini Interview for Medical School: Practice Interview Series Exam 2 by Jordan Westley

Multiple Mini Interview for Medical School: Practice Interview Series Exam 3 by Jordan Westley

More Resources

Medical School Multiple Mini Interview: The Essentials
By Jordan Westley

The multiple mini interview can be made into a very complicated and stressful event. There are an infinite number of possible questions and scenarios. This book strives to simplify the multiple mini interview. Understand the interview from the interviewer's perspective. Learn an approach so you feel comfortable and confident in answering any question. Distillation of the MMI to the essence keeps it simple in your mind. This results in less chance of error during the stress of the interview. Practice with practice interview questions designed to simulate the real MMI. Knowledge and practice to help you answer interview questions with ease and confidence.

www.ingramcontent.com/pod-product-compliance
Lightning Source LLC
Chambersburg PA
CBHW030226170426
43194CB00007BA/876